NATIONAL PARKS

ZION

Erinn Banting

www.av2books.com

Step 1
Go to **www.av2books.com**

Step 2
Enter this unique code

AHTKYDA94

Step 3
Explore your interactive eBook!

CONTENTS

AV2 is optimized for use on any device

Your interactive eBook comes with...

Contents
Browse a live contents page to easily navigate through resources

Audio
Listen to sections of the book read aloud

Videos
Watch informative video clips

Weblinks
Gain additional information for research

Try This!
Complete activities and hands-on experiments

Key Words
Study vocabulary, and complete a matching word activity

Quizzes
Test your knowledge

Slideshows
View images and captions

... and much, much more!

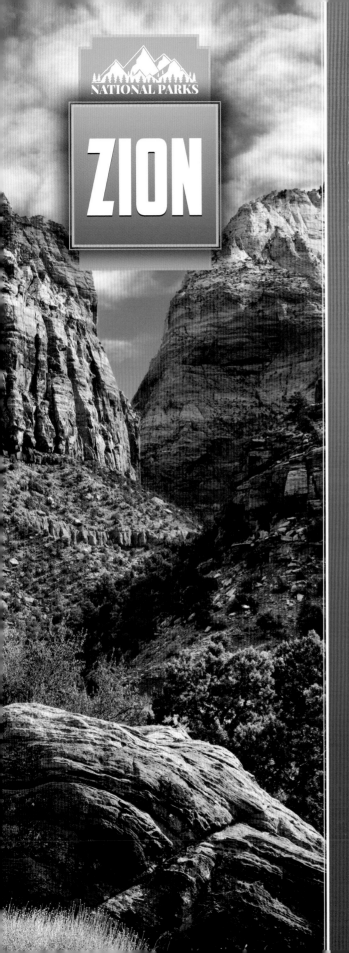

NATIONAL PARKS

ZION

CONTENTS

A sandstone wonder

Zion National Park, in southern Utah, is known for its sandstone canyons and breathtaking views. It is also home to some of the most unique rock formations, plants, and wildlife in the United States. More than 4 million people visit the park every year to take in its 229 square miles (593 square kilometers) of rugged beauty.

Two large canyons, Zion and Kolob, run through Zion National Park. These canyons make up the park's two main areas. Each area contains diverse landscapes. These include desert ranges, lush valleys, and the coniferous forests that cover some of the park's highest peaks.

Zion National Park was established on **November 19, 1919**.

The park contains more than **100 miles** (161 km) of hiking trails.

Zion Canyon is **15 miles** (24 km) **long** and **3,000 feet** (914 meters) **deep**.

The Great White Throne looms 2,394 feet (730 m) above the Zion Canyon floor. It is considered the symbol of Zion National Park.

The park's tallest peak is found in the Kolob Canyon area. Called Horse Ranch Mountain, it stands 8,726 feet (2,660 m) high. In the Zion Canyon area, visitors can climb 1,488 feet (454 m) to the top of Angels Landing. This is one of the best places to take in the park's natural beauty.

Angels Landing is considered an iconic, but strenuous, hike. Those who reach the summit are rewarded with stunning views of the park.

MAPPING ZION

NEVADA

Salt Lake City •

UTAH

• Cedar City

• Springdale

ARIZONA

LEGEND
N
☐ Land
▨ Zion National Park
• City

MAP SCALE 0 |⊢—————| 60 Miles
|⊢—————|
60 Km

Where Is Zion?

Zion National Park is located in Utah's southwest corner. The park sits along the western edge of the Colorado **Plateau**. This plateau extends through western Colorado, northwestern New Mexico, southern and eastern Utah, and northern Arizona. Zion is surrounded by highlands. To its west are the Pine Valley Mountains. Kolob Terrace lies to the northeast. Hurricane Terrace forms the park's southern boundary.

Zion is one of the most-visited national parks in the United States. It can be easily accessed from the large cities found nearby. The park is 320 miles (515 km) southwest of Salt Lake City, Utah, and 166 miles (267 km) northeast of Las Vegas, Nevada. The town closest to the park is Springdale, Utah. It lies 1.1 miles (1.8 km) to the south.

...s Zion's main gateway town. To serve the millions of ...ass through every year, the town has built numerous ...ants, and gift shops along its main roads.

PUZZLER

Parts of Zion National Park are covered in desert. Deserts are one of the world's major types of **biomes**. Approximately 20 percent of Earth's surface is covered by deserts.

Q: There are four major deserts in North America. Can you identify each desert on the map below?

CANADA

HINT: This 190,000-square mile (492,098-sq. km) desert is the largest in the United States.

UNITED STATES

Pacific Ocean

HINT: Telescope Peak and Death Valley are located in this desert.

HINT: The Rio Grande crosses this desert.

Gulf of Mexico

Hint: This desert is the only place in the world where the saguaro cactus grows.

MEXICO

ANSWERS: A. Great Basin B. Mojave C. Sonoran D. Chihuahuan

A Trip Back in Time

The deep layers of rock found in Zion National Park took millions of years to form. Approximately 240 million years ago, the area was a flat basin. Streams ran from nearby mountains into this basin. Their waters contained sand, rocks, and other **sediments** that had **eroded** from the mountains. These sediments formed layers within the basin. Over time, their weight caused the land to sink.

Water carrying minerals trickled through the layers of sediment. The minerals acted like cement and glued the sediments together. This process, called lithification, turned the sediments into rock.

Over the past 80 million years, movement deep underground has pushed up the Colorado Plateau. The rock layers have become exposed to wind, rain, and flowing rivers. These forces have worked to erode the rock. This has helped to form the canyons, cliffs, and rock formations found in the park today.

Most of the rock in Zion National Park is sedimentary, with sandstone being the most visible type of rock.

CARVED THROUGH TIME

The **geologic** processes that took place millions of years ago created the nine distinct rock layers now found in Zion National Park.

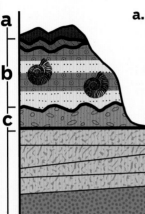

a. Cedar Mountain Formation This rock and sandstone layer was formed approximately 120 million years ago. It is most visible at the top of Horse Ranch Mountain.

b. Carmel Formation Formed between 165 and 170 million years ago, this limestone layer contains **fossils** of marine animals that once lived in the area.

c. Temple Cap Formation Made up of sandstone and mudstone, this layer formed between 170 and 175 million years ago.

d. Navajo Sandstone This sandstone layer came from a vast desert that covered the region between 180 and 185 million years ago.

e. Kayenta Formation This sandstone and mudstone layer was created between 185 and 195 million years ago, before the region dried into a desert.

f. Moenave Formation Fossils of dinosaur footprints can be found in this layer. It formed between 195 and 210 million years ago.

g. Chinle Formation Formed between 210 and 225 million years ago, this layer includes ash from volcanoes that erupted within the Colorado Plateau.

h. Moenkopi Formation Made up of mudstone, sandstone, siltstone, and limestone, this layer formed between 240 and 250 million years ago.

i. Kaibab Formation The limestone and siltstone in this layer date back approximately 270 million years.

Zion's Plant Life

More than 1,000 types of plants can be found in Zion National Park. One of the most common flowers is the sacred datura. Nicknamed the "Zion lily," its large white flowers are 5 to 8 inches (13 to 20 centimeters) long.

Natural hanging gardens grow in places where water streams down cliff walls. The gardens are made up of a variety of plants. Flowers such as golden columbines, Zion shooting stars, and scarlet monkey flowers add a burst of color. Mosses provide a lush green background.

Pine, fir, and aspen trees can be found at higher elevations. Ponderosa pines can grow up to 130 feet (40 m) tall. They have orange bark that smells like vanilla. Plants such as yucca and cholla grow on the park's desert floor. Pinyon, cliffrose, and mesquite are other plants that grow well in these lower, warmer parts of the park.

...ura is one of the most dangerous plants in ...ark. Every part of it is poisonous, and it has ...se of several human deaths.

ZION'S PLANT COMMUNITIES

Zion National Park's elevation ranges from 3,700 to 8,700 feet (1,128 to 2,652 m). Having such a wide range means that the park can support a variety of plants. The park is home to several plant communities. Each is found in an area that best meets its needs for growth.

Riparian Plants such as ferns, grasses, wildflowers, and aquatic plants need a regular supply of water. They can be found growing along the banks of the Virgin River and in its nearby wetlands.

Arid Grasslands Shrubs, cacti, and grasses live at the park's lower elevations. These plants are able to withstand the high temperatures and minimal rainfall found here.

Pinyon-Juniper Forest This type of forest is located at higher elevations of the desert. The pinyon pines and juniper trees of this forest have **adapted** to cope with both cold temperatures and drought conditions.

Ponderosa Pine These trees grow high on canyon cliffs. They survive cold temperatures and strong winds by growing deep roots into the sandstone cliffs and canyons.

Mixed Conifer Forest This type of forest grows at the park's higher elevations. It features Douglas firs and white pines, as well as ponderosa pines.

Zion's Wildlife

Zion's diverse landscapes provide **habitats** for hundreds of wildlife **species**. The park's lower areas are home to birds ranging from wild turkeys to warblers. The California condor can be seen at higher elevations. With a wingspan of 9 to 10 feet (2.74 to 3 m), it is the largest flying bird in North America.

Larger mammals in the park include mountain lions and mule deer. Bighorn sheep live in the park's lower regions, but their rubber-like hooves allow them to climb to higher ground. Smaller mammals found in the park include rock squirrels and kangaroo rats.

Reptiles, such as the collared lizard, can be seen sunning themselves in canyons. Amphibians, such as frogs and toads, are often found along the park's riverbanks. Fish swimming in the Virgin River include the speckled dace and desert sucker.

The collared lizard is one of 16 lizard species in Zion National Park. It can be identified by the two black bands of color on its shoulder and neck.

MEXICAN SPOTTED OWL

National parks provide an opportunity for people to see a wide variety of wildlife. They also help to protect **endangered** species and those that are under threat of becoming endangered. The Mexican spotted owl is one such species. Protected throughout the United States, it can be found in the forests and canyons of Zion National Park.

The Mexican spotted owl is considered a threatened animal in both the United States and Mexico. Its numbers are declining mainly due to habitat loss. People are cutting down the trees the owls rely on for shelter. It is estimated that there are only about 2,100 Mexican spotted owls living in the entire United States.

The Mexican spotted owl is one of the largest owls in North America. It can be up to 19 inches (48 centimeters) in length, and have a wingspan of up to 45 inches (114 cm).

A Rich History

Native Americans lived in the Zion National Park area long before settlers arrived. When a group of **Mormons** came to settle the land in the 1850s, they were helped by the Southern Paiute people. The land was difficult, but the Mormons were amazed by the scenic beauty around them. They called the area *Zion*. This is the Hebrew word for "**sanctuary**."

In 1872, the U.S. government sent John Wesley Powell to **survey** the area. To show respect to the Southern Paiute, he named the land *Mukuntuweap*. This means "straight canyon" in the Paiute language. The name refers to the tall, straight walls of the area's canyons.

In 1904, a painting by Frederick S. Dellenbaugh was displayed at the World's Fair in St. Louis. It showed the natural beauty of the Zion area. Visitors came to the site in droves. President Taft acknowledged its importance by declaring Mukuntuweap a national monument in 1909.

...gan arriving in the area now known as ...iginally from Illinois, they moved west in ...e place to practice their religious beliefs.

The name was changed to Zion National Monument by Horace Albright, director of the National Park Service, in 1918. He thought changing the name would attract even more tourists. The following year, Zion National Park was officially established. It was to be Utah's first national park.

BIOGRAPHY

Gilbert Stanley Underwood (1890–1960)

Gilbert Stanley Underwood showed an early interest in architecture. By the time he was 20, he was already working as a **draftsperson** for other architects. It was during this time that he learned about a style called "arts and crafts." Buildings in this style were made using natural materials.

Underwood used this style to design many structures for the National Park System. One of these buildings was Zion Lodge. Designed in 1924, the lodge was built in the heart of Zion Canyon. Its **rustic** style was created using stone and lumber. This allowed the lodge to blend in with its surroundings. Zion Lodge was destroyed in a fire in 1966, but was rebuilt in 1990 to look like the original. Today, the lodge is once again a popular resting stop for people visiting the park.

FACTS OF LIFE

Born: 1890

Hometown: Oneida, New York

Occupation: Architect

Died: 1960

Zion Lodge is the only hotel within the park.

THE BIG PICTURE

Over millions of years, forces below and above ground shaped the spectacular rock formations in Zion National Park. The Kolob Arch, which is 287 feet (87 m) long, is one of the largest freestanding arches on Earth. Fascinating rock formations come in many shapes and sizes. They can be found all over the world.

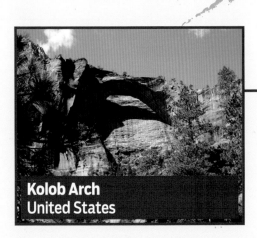

Kolob Arch
United States

North
America

Atlantic
Ocean

Pacific
Ocean

South
America

Valley of the Moon
Argentina

Southern
Ocean

LEGEND

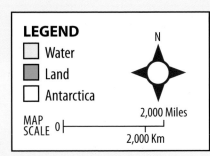

- ☐ Water
- ☐ Land
- ☐ Antarctica

N

MAP
SCALE 0 ├─────────┤ 2,000 Miles
            2,000 Km

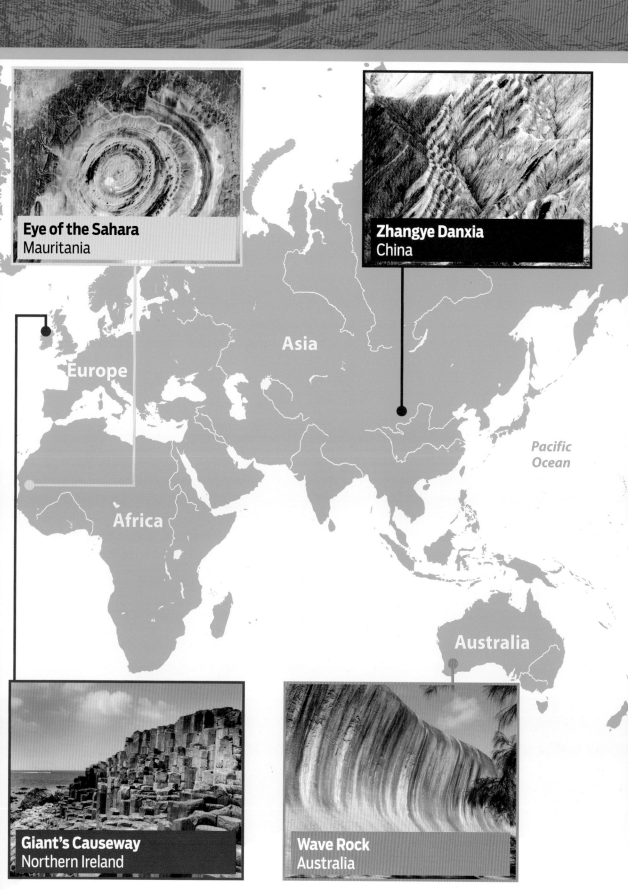

Eye of the Sahara
Mauritania

Zhangye Danxia
China

Asia

Europe

Africa

Pacific
Ocean

Australia

Giant's Causeway
Northern Ireland

Wave Rock
Australia

Antarctica

People of the Colorado Plateau

People have lived in the area now known as Zion National Park for at least 12,000 years. **Archaeologists** have found spear tips from that time in the area. The people who used them would have hunted **Ice Age** species, such as woolly mammoths.

Other Aboriginal groups, such as the Virgin Anasazi and Parowan Fremont, came later. They hunted and farmed the land for hundreds of years. Drought and flooding finally forced these groups to leave the region.

In about 1100 AD, the Paiute, Shoshone, and Goshute peoples moved into the area. They hunted animals and gathered seeds and nuts. The Southern Paiute also planted crops such as corn and squash. They used hand-woven baskets to gather food and store their crops. The baskets were so tightly woven they could carry water.

The Paiute, Shoshone, and Goshute still live in the area today. They have been joined by the Ute and the Navajo. All of these groups continue to preserve and honor the traditions of their **ancestors**.

People can hike to Petroglyph Canyon to see the rock drawings of Zion's early Aboriginal Peoples. The site contains more than 150 individual drawings. They are believed to be more than 1,000 years old.

PUZZLER

Early Aboriginal Peoples relied on the natural resources they found in and around what is now Zion National Park. The Anasazi made stone containers that they sealed with mud. They used these containers to preserve their food. The Paiute were so skilled at making stone spear tips and arrowheads that they traded them with neighboring peoples.

Q. Why were stones and rocks used to make such a wide variety of items?

ANSWER: These materials were easy for the Aboriginal Peoples to find in the area.

TIMELINE

10,000 BC
The first humans use the area as a hunting ground.

240 million years ago
A shallow basin covers the area that is now Zion National Park. Nearby waters flow sediments into it.

1850

500 AD

10,000 BC

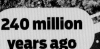

240 million years ago

240–120 million years ago
The layers of sediment become rock through the process of lithification.

1850s
Mormon settlers arrive in the area and call it Zion.

500 AD
The first permanent settlements in the area are built by the Anasazi.

1956
The Kolob Canyon area is made part of Zion National Park.

2019
Zion National Park celebrates its 100th anniversary.

1900

1950

2000

2050

1919
Zion National Park is established as Utah's first national park.

1872
John Wesley Powell explores and surveys the region.

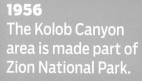

2009
President Obama signs the Omnibus Public Land Management Act, which increases the size of the park.

OVERCROWDING

Millions of people visit Zion National Park each year. The number of visitors has increased over time. This has led to overcrowding, one of the major issues facing the park. The park is not currently set up to handle the garbage and waste these people produce. This is creating an unhealthy environment for both visitors and the park's wildlife.

Wildlife is also being affected by people who want to experience nature away from the crowds. Hikers often go off marked trails. Campers sometimes set up campsites in restricted areas. Their actions damage the natural environment and disrupt the wildlife that live within it.

Zion's shuttle system has been in operation since 2000. In 2017 alone, it transported more than 6.3 million riders.

Should Zion National Park put a cap on visitors?

Yes	No
The National Park Service is responsible for protecting Zion's many natural wonders. A cap would reduce the damage done to the natural environment.	National parks are established so that people can explore and learn about the country's many natural wonders. The cap might discourage people from visiting Zion.
If fewer people were allowed into the park, the issues relating to overcrowding would be reduced. Waste could be disposed of properly. Campgrounds and hiking trails could be better monitored.	The National Park Service relies on entrance fees to run and maintain the park. Fewer visitors would mean less money for the park.

Zion National Park has many programs in place to help protect the park. To reduce plastic waste, filling stations have been set up around the park. They provide free water for visitors, allowing them to reuse their water bottles instead of throwing them away. To control the flow of people and traffic, the park started a shuttle bus system. During the busy summer season, visitors must use the shuttle to access certain parts of the park.

However, the park continues to struggle to control the overcrowding problem. Recently, there has been talk of putting a cap on visitors. This would limit the number of people who could

Natural Attractions

Zion National Park has much to offer its visitors. The park has trails to hike, rocks to climb, and several scenic drives. No matter how people choose to explore the park, there are many sights to see.

The Zion-Mount Carmel Highway can be traveled by car or shuttle. The road goes through the Zion-Mount Carmel Tunnel. When it was built in 1930, it was the longest tunnel of its kind in the United States. Rock formations such as the White Cliffs and Great Arch of Zion can be seen from this highway as well.

The shuttle also travels along the Canyon Scenic Drive. The Great White Throne and Angels Landing can be seen along this route. Visitors can hop off at any time to explore hiking trails such as Weeping Rock and the Emerald Pools. Climbing spots along the shuttle route include Mount Isaac and Cable Mountain.

One of the more challenging hikes in the park is The Subway. The trail runs through a narrow canyon and features several waterfalls and pools.

PREPARATION IS KEY

A visit to Zion National Park is a great way to spend a day outdoors. It is important to bring supplies and stay safe while enjoying the landscapes and wildlife in the park. Visitors must remember to stay on marked trails and keep a safe distance from all animals.

Wear a hat, sunglasses, and clothing that is appropriate for the weather.

Put on sunscreen and insect repellent.

Bring a water bottle you can use at one of the filling stations.

Pack snacks.

Bring a camera and binoculars.

Carry a flashlight, or bring a headlamp.

Wear comfortable shoes or boots.

A Natural Heritage

The land now known as Zion National Park provided early Aboriginal Peoples with everything they needed to survive. The rivers and streams supplied them with food and fish. The canyons gave them shelter. Pots were made using clay and mud. Reeds and grasses became baskets. Aboriginal Peoples even looked to the land to explain how they came to be. These stories have been passed from one generation to the next.

Today, Aboriginal Peoples in the area continue to preserve the traditions of their ancestors. One way they do this is by holding powwows. These celebrations showcase traditional Aboriginal ways. People dress in clothing that reflects the past. They play drums and perform dances that honor both their ancestors and the land. Aboriginal arts and crafts, such as baskets and jewelry, are put on display.

Powwows often last several days. They include Aboriginal Peoples from different nations and various parts of the country.

ZION MYTHOLOGY

Sinawava, or the coyote, is an important figure in Paiute **mythology**. In one story, Sinawava leaves his home in America and travels east toward the rising Sun. Sinawava makes a new home for himself. He marries and has many children. These children are said to be the ancestors of the Aboriginal Peoples of North and South America.

According to the myth, Sinawava decided to return to America. He put his children into a wosa, a woven jug with a cork, so he could carry them home. On the way, Sinawava heard his children playing drums and singing inside the wosa. When he reached the American east cost, he decided to check on them. He opened the jug. All but two of his children ran out from the wosa. They spread out across both North and South America.

When Sinawava reached his homeland, he released the other two children. They are said to be the ancestors of the Shoshone and Paiute peoples who live in Utah, Nevada, Idaho, California, and Oregon today.

WHAT HAVE YOU LEARNED?

TRUE OR FALSE?

Decide whether the following statements are true or false. If the statement is false, make it true.

1 Horse Ranch Mountain is the tallest peak in Zion National Park.

2 There are more than 10,000 types of plants in Zion National Park.

3 The California condor is the largest flying bird in the world.

4 The Southern Paiute used baskets to carry food, hold water, and store crops.

5 President Kennedy declared Mukuntuweap a national monument in 1909.

6 Overcrowding is one of the major issues facing Zion National Park.

ANSWERS
1. True
2. False. There are more than 1,000 types of plants.
3. False. It is the largest flying bird in North America.
4. True.
5. False. President Taft declared it a monument.
6. True.

SHORT ANSWER

Answer the following questions using information from the book.

1 Which rock formation is considered the symbol of Zion National Park?

2 What is the sacred datura nicknamed?

3 Who designed the Zion Lodge in 1924?

4 What are two rock formations that can be seen when traveling on the Zion-Mount Carmel Highway?

5 In what year was Zion National Park established?

MULTIPLE CHOICE

Choose the best answer for the following questions.

1 In which state is Zion National Park located?

a. Florida
b. Utah
c. Alaska

2 What does Zion mean in Hebrew?

a. Desert
b. Beautiful
c. Sanctuary

3 In which year was Frederick S. Dellenbaugh's painting on display at the St. Louis World's Fair?

a. 1904
b. 2001
c. 1845

4 What percentage of Earth's surface is covered by desert?

a. 20
b. 5
c. 80

SEDIMENTARY ROCK SNACK

Sedimentary rocks are formed when layers of material are deposited and harden. With an adult's help, try this activity to see how sedimentary rocks are formed.

Materials

4 tablespoons (60 milliliters) unsalted butter

3 cups (710 mL) mini marshmallows

3 cups (710 mL) rice cereal

1 teaspoon (5 mL) vanilla extract

Mini chocolate chips

Chocolate or gummy candies

A saucepan

A nonstick muffin tin

Instructions

1. Melt the butter and marshmallows in the saucepan.

2. When the mixture is smooth, add the vanilla extract.

3. Stir in the rice cereal.

4. Take half of the mixture and press it into the muffin tin cups.

5. Sprinkle a layer of mini chocolate chips on top of each mixture.

6. Put the rest of the rice cereal mixture on top of that layer.

7. Sprinkle candies on top.

8. Press down firmly to make sure the layers are all stuck together. Let the mixture cool.

9. Remove the snacks from the tin cups. How many layers do you see? How does making your snack compare to the creation of sedimentary rock?

10. Enjoy your snack while you compare the two processes.

KEY WORDS

adapted: underwent changes to survive in an environment

ancestors: relatives who lived in the past

archaeologists: people who study the remains of past human life

biomes: areas where specific animals and plants live

draftsperson: someone who draws plans and sketches for a living

endangered: at risk of no longer living on Earth

eroded: worn away by the action of water, wind, or glacial ice

fossils: the remains of living things that are preserved from a past age

geologic: relating to the study of Earth's rocks and minerals

habitats: places where plants and animals live and grow

Ice Age: a period in Earth's history when sheets of ice covered large areas of the planet

Mormons: members of the Church of Jesus Christ of Latter-day Saints

mythology: stories about ancient times or natural events

plateau: an area of level, high ground

rustic: made in a plain and simple fashion

sanctuary: a safe place

sediments: materials deposited by water, wind, or glaciers

species: a specific group of plants or animals that shares characteristics

survey: to examine and record the features of an area of land

INDEX

Get the best of both worlds.

AV2 bridges the gap between print and digital.

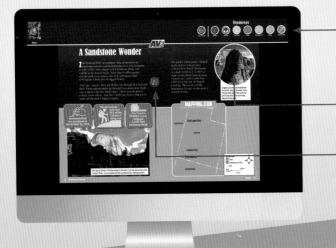

The expandable resources toolbar enables quick access to content including **videos**, **audio**, **activities**, **weblinks**, **slideshows**, **quizzes**, and **key words**.

Animated videos make static images come alive.

Resource icons on each page help readers to further **explore key concepts**.

Published by AV2
350 5th Avenue, 59th Floor
New York, NY 10118
Website: www.av2books.com

Library of Congress Cataloging-in-Publication Data
Names: Banting, Erinn, author.
Title: Zion / Erinn Banting and Heather Kissock.
Description: New York, NY : AV2, [2021] | Series: National Parks | Includes index. | Audience: Ages 10-12. | Audience: Grades 4-6. |
    Summary: "National Parks leads young readers on a journey through some of the best-known national parks in the United States. Each
    book in the series teaches readers geography skills and reveals fascinating facts"-- Provided by publisher.
Identifiers: LCCN 2019039035 (print) | LCCN 2019039036 (ebook) | ISBN 9781791116040 (library binding) | ISBN 9781791116057
    (paperback) | ISBN 9781791116064 (multi-user eBook) | ISBN 9781791116071 (single-user eBook)
Subjects: LCSH: Zion National Park (Utah)--Juvenile literature.
Classification: LCC F832.Z8 B36 2021 (print) | LCC F832.Z8 (ebook) | DDC 979.2/48--dc23
LC record available at https://lccn.loc.gov/2019039035
LC ebook record available at https://lccn.loc.gov/2019039036

Printed in Guangzhou, China
1 2 3 4 5 6 7 8 9 0 24 23 22 21 20

012020
101319

Project Coordinator Heather Kissock
Designers Tammy West, Ana Maria Vidal, and Terry Paulhus
Captions Heather Kissock

Photo Credits
Every reasonable effort has been made to trace ownership and to obtain permission to reprint copyright material. The publishers would be pleased to have any errors or omissions brought to their attention so that they may be corrected in subsequent printings. AV2 acknowledges Getty Images, Alamy, Shutterstock, and Heather Kissock as its primary photo suppliers for this title.